THE DEFENCE OF BLOODFORD VILLAGE

COLONEL G. A. WADE M.C.

The Naval & Military Press Ltd

Published by

The Naval & Military Press Ltd
Unit 10 Ridgewood Industrial Park,
Uckfield, East Sussex,
TN22 5QE England

Tel: +44 (0) 1825 749494
Fax: +44 (0) 1825 765701

www.naval-military-press.com
www.nmarchive.com

FOREWORD

" The Battle of Bloodford Village and how it came to be successfully defended as a result of the lessons learnt from the dreams of the local Home Guard Commander, makes most interesting and instructive reading.

" The story contains many useful hints that should help other Home Guard Commanders in planning the defence of their villages."

Director General Home Guard.

28th November, 1940.

"THE DEFENCE OF BLOODFORD VILLAGE."

It is a strange thought that the whole course of history can be changed by the habits of one unknown individual—Yet it is so. And who shall say that the Home Guard's magnificent defence of the now famous village of BLOODFORD, holding up the German advance for the critical hours which lost them the battle of Britain, had not a decisive effect upon the War ? The name of Geoffrey Gee, known affectionately as " Skipper Gee," has taken its place amongst the immortals directly because of his incurable habit of eating highly-indigestible suppers which gave rise to dreams of an extraordinarily vivid kind.

Point No. 1.

CULTIVATE A TACTICAL EYE FOR COUNTRY

Wherever you go make a careful note of the features of the Countryside, they all have fighting value.

You should know every hill, every road, every lane, every wood, every ditch and every bit of cover in your area.

This will give you an immense advantage over any invader and may save your life sometime.

In view of its world-wide fame it seems almost unnecessary to describe BLOODFORD, but for a clear understanding of what follows this is a brief description :—

Situated in the bend of the River BOOZE this beautiful little village of 500 inhabitants is on ground which rises towards the NORTH and falls away to the SOUTH. The quaint old houses are grouped round a large village green upon which still stands the Old Gibbet. At HAG'S POND on the EAST side of the village there is the original old Ducking Stool. These relics of the past make three battered German tanks standing on the Green look out of place somehow, and yet the Bloodford Home Guard, who captured them, would start another War rather than let them go.

A picturesque feature is WINDMILL HILL upon which stands the old Windmill which has looked down upon the village for 300 years. A lane running due SOUTH leads to FORD FARM which is close to the Ford over the River BOOZE. It was the sanguinary combat between Britons and Romans for the possession of this ford which gave the village its name.

Three roads run out of the village, NORTH to WALLOP, EAST to POPPIT and WEST, over the River, to BEATIT. There are two luxuriant woods close to the village—OAK WOOD and PINE WOOD. CUT BROOK, a small tributary of the River BOOZE, winds its way on the SOUTH-EAST. This lively little stream must have flowed for countless generations to cut its banks away so steeply. In summer it is the favourite Lovers' Walk for the villagers, but in winter it sometimes overflows its banks and makes the fields near the river very marshy. Before you leave the village you should go along the BEATIT road till you come to the Bridge ; you will see a large house with a walled garden on the North side of the road. This is Skipper Gee's house, The Grange, and you will see it has been repaired a lot. The Bridge Inn is the last building and is on the River Bank close to the Bridge, and just across the road are the old stables with their lofts overlooking the Bridge and river. The Bridge and the old Inn with its half timbering, lichened roof, and swinging Sign make a delightful picture. Examining the Sign closely you will see it bears the Arms of the Bloodford Family (now extinct, the male members having all died young) and their motto RIVULUS CUM AQUA FLUIT can just be distinguished. The translation is " LET THE RIVER FLOW LIKE WATER," which, as the local inhabitants point out with pride, only makes sense in the case of this particular river.

When finally you go back to contemplate this historic spot from WINDMILL HILL, gazing down into its peaceful square, seeing the blue smoke curling up lazily from its chimneys, you will find it difficult to realize that only a few short months ago Hell was let loose upon this little village and deeds of skill and daring were done in its defence which will be remembered for all time. And those deeds, mark you, were done not by trained men of the Regular Army, but by members of the Village's own Home Guard, who left their work at a moment's notice, took up weapons and decisively defeated an enemy infinitely better armed.

But now back to Skipper Gee and his dreams, or rather, NIGHTMARES!

He was appointed to command the Bloodford Company of the Home Guard, because the local men liked and respected him.

On the first Saturday afternoon following his appointment Skipper Gee held a parade of his entire force and very fine they looked. Two-thirds of them had rifles, some had shot guns and all had Denim overalls. Whereas some seemed desperately anxious to recapture the smartness of twenty years before, others were eager to learn the A.B.C. of Soldiering. Their faces registered determination and Gee had a proud feeling that, well handled, these men would face up to anything or anybody. About eighty men were on parade and the roll call was interesting because most of the men, being villagers, responded to nicknames, called out quite seriously.

No. 1 Platoon was commanded by the village lawyer known as " Snowgood " Phease, owing to his habit of always saying " It's no good " whenever one of his clients wanted to go to Court (thereby saving them much money). No. 2 Platoon was commanded by " Windy " Sugden. In justice be it stated that ex-Sergeant Sugden won the M.M. during the last war, being nicknamed " Windy " merely on account of his general talkativeness, and No. 3 Platoon by " Guesser " Ferrit, an old poacher now Game Keeper employed by the local squire.

After the Inspection Skipper Gee addressed the Home Guard, warned them of their responsibilities and asked them to work hard to improve their knowledge of soldiering. This all the Guards enthusiastically undertook to do and Gee went home pondering deeply on his job. All evening he worked hard on a Defence Scheme for the village which interested him so deeply that the Church clock had chimed midnight before he ate a large piece of cheese and went to bed. Soon after putting out the light he had the first of those terrible dreams out of which the defences of Bloodford were to evolve towards perfection.

In the first, as in all others, Skipper Gee found himself the helpless spectator of a drama which unfolded itself before his anguished gaze and in which, in spite of the utmost effort, he was powerless to intervene.

DREAM NUMBER ONE

It was early morning, patches of mist still hung on the Village Green, the sun rising over OAK WOOD was reflected in the water of HAG'S POND and sundry roosters proclaimed the birth of another day. No one could be seen in the streets although the rattle of buckets and the clank of the pumps showed that early risers were astir. " The best time of the day," thought Gee, " when the larks are singing and the sky is such a lovely deep blue, and —My God! What's that ? " for floating downwards were some tiny white specks. " Parachutists !—Yes, eight of them, and look there's a score of them over there as well ! " In agony Gee looked round. Why didn't somebody *do something* ? They would come to earth only a mile away and be here in no time and yet still the buckets were rattling and the men whistling and the cocks crowing just as though DEATH was not advancing from two directions at once !

Looking wildly round he saw to his great relief " Windy Sugden " come to his gate and stand gazing contentedly round the sunlit square. Gee tried to yell but no sound came. He tried to run but could not move. He could only wait in utter anguish while Windy turned, without so much as a glance into the sky, and went to the cowshed. The parachutists were nearly down now and Gee knew well enough that soon, heavily armed and merciless, they would be converging on the unsuspecting village, their minds set on MURDER, PILLAGE and RAPE.

What was that ? Shots ! Not a very unusual sound in this sporting country, and no one took any notice.

Then came a tinkle-tinkle-tinkle getting gradually louder and louder and coming from the WALLOP ROAD. A boy on a bicycle, wild with excitement, pedalling furiously and ringing his bell all the time, streaked into the square, fell from the cycle, picked himself up and yelled :—" Murder ! Murder ! Murder ! Germans ! Germans ! Parachutes ! Parachutes ! hundreds ! and hundreds ! Help ! Help ! "

Doors opened, men, women and children dashed out of houses, surrounded him and gazed unbelievingly into the sky. Windy Sugden rushed up, seized the frantic boy, shook him roughly and was about to question him when the lad crumpled up and fell in a heap. Opening his shirt Windy started back in horror ; and silence descended instantly on the excited group, for on the small white chest was a red, trickling bullet hole.
' At last " (thought Gee bitterly) " they realize the Germans are here ! "

Point No. 2.
AT ALL TIMES GUARD AGAINST SURPRISE
This is the FIRST DUTY of a soldier, not to be caught on the hop.

Every Home Guard should know exactly what to do on alarm and should be prepared to do it smoothly and quietly whatever unexpected happening may take place.

" Stand to, the Home Guard ! " yelled Windy Sugden in a voice which rang round the square—" Ring the Church Bells "—" Get out the carts for the Road Blocks ! " Other voices were calling " Who has got the key of the Ammunition Store ? " " Burst the door in someone ! " " Where does No. 2 Platoon fall in ? " " I can't find the matches for the Molotoff Cocktails ! " Just as the Church Bells started to ring (after many months, silence) Gee was not surprised to see himself rush out of his house with a rifle in one hand and a Denim suit in the other, and go over to where the Home Guard was falling in on the Green.

And then Gee saw something which filled him with cold dread—the glint of steel helmets in the far corner of the square. There was the rat—tat-tat—tat—tat of a machine gun and soon the Home Guard lay in one palpitating heap with their wives and children mixed with them. Gee saw himself load his rifle, aim at the advancing Germans and bowl over first one, then another and then—but look out ! Germans who had advanced from the other side of the square had crept up behind and struck him savagely on the head ! Swarms of Boches were now tearing like madmen through the houses and shots and screams sounded in all directions.

Soon a deadly calm reigned and Gee saw himself a prisoner between two soldiers being taken before an Officer who asked " Why were you fighting against us without a uniform or armlet ? " Gee heard himself say : " I had not time to put it on ! " and in the chorus of laughter which followed Gee saw the Officer wave his hand in the direction of the famous Gibbet ; saw himself put against the wall and ruthlessly shot. When he saw his own body hoisted high on the old gibbet Gee felt the climax of horror had been reached.

At breakfast next morning Skipper Gee, who was limp and tired, was suddenly startled by his daughter saying " Good Heavens, Daddy, don't look at me like that, you have got an expression like a Dictator being photographed ! "

As a matter of fact every time the Skipper contemplated her sweet, fresh face his mind wandered to his dream of the night before and he kept asking himself " Was the dream so fantastic after all ? " " Was *any part* of it such that it could not really happen ? Had not things like this *already happened* in this War ? Would he not be a blind fool to assume that it would not happen in Bloodford ? " And like a flash he realized how heavy was his responsibility as Commander of the Home Guard, how paramount his duty to prevent such tragedies.

He realized that previous to this dream he had been playing with the job but now he would tackle it in deadly earnest, and in the days which followed he arranged a lookout post on the top of the Old Windmill, carefully detailing the Guards to man it, saw that a regular roster was kept and a code of signals was arranged and the men practised in giving the alarm. Some were inclined to think he was exaggerating things but soon all of them were infected by his air of absolute certainty that the enemy would come and took their tasks very seriously. Every moment which could be spared from their work was devoted by the Home Guard to drill, musketry, making Molotoff Cocktails and rehearsing the occupation of the outpost positions. The disposition of his men was finally as shown on Map No. 1.

Skipper Gee would have liked one or two more posts but the points to be occupied took up all his men. As he lay in bed turning things over in his mind before going to sleep he said " We seem to be pretty well covered all round," and then a little later came :—

DREAM NUMBER TWO
Everything was going finely. The lookout on WINDMILL HILL had spotted the enemy ; the alarm had been given in good time and the Home Guard had paraded swiftly and smoothly. Already the post at DUCK INN had killed five parachutists who had come from OAK WOOD. Gee had been torn with anxiety when he saw the Germans advancing for fear fire would be opened too soon and the enemy escape back to the Wood ; but the little garrison at DUCK INN kept as still as statues till the Huns were so close that the first burst of fire swept EVERY BOCHE off his feet and not one even kicked afterwards.

Point No. 5.

HOLD YOUR FIRE

In nine cases out of ten it will pay you to hold your fire till an advancing enemy is so close that you cannot miss. If you open fire too soon, he may take cover and escape.

Remember, countless splendid opportunities have been lost in warfare simply because someone opened fire too soon.

Eight of the enemy in a captured lorry had tried to rush the road block by the Church Yard and old Guesser Ferrit who was hidden behind a tombstone bearing the exhortation " LEAD KINDLY LIGHT ! " had thrown a Molotoff Cocktail slap amongst the enemy and had chased one who was ablaze right back to the bridge, finally hurling him into the river. The other Germans, blackened and burnt, had been captured by the members of the Road Block Guard. Hearing more firing from the S.W. Gee, saw some advancing Germans hesitate before the BULL FARM POST and then run back to PINE WOOD. In great delight he saw his defences holding everywhere and he thought the battle would soon be over.

It was ; for hearing a loud sound from the South he was just in time to see a light Tank splashing across the ford in a fountain of spray and foam. The piquet at FORD FARM fired a few ineffective shots as the Tank sped up the lane and with a thrill of apprehension Gee suddenly recollected that the lane entered the Village *behind* the road block !

Point No. 6.

STUDY THE ROAD BLOCKS

Make sure they block **every** road into the Village. They should be placed where the enemy comes on them unexpectedly and where they can be defended by A. W. Bombs or Molotoff Cocktails, preferably from an upstairs window but failing that, from a slit trench.

The defensive points, in addition to completely covering Road Blocks with fire, should always be capable of all-round defence because if the Block stops an enemy vehicle, an attempt will at once be made to push men round the flanks of the Defenders to take them in the rear.

In stupefied horror he watched the Tank reach the square, fire a burst up POPPIT ROAD killing the Road Block Guard who were looking in the opposite direction, and career on towards the Church Road Block. Here the entire garrison were bunched together talking over their victory and congratulating Guesser Ferrit on his exploit. Gee saw the whole lot bowled over even before the sound of the machine gun reached him. He saw old Guesser get up again and with blood spouting down his face advance towards the Tank with fists clenched, but only for a few yards, then another blast of fire struck him and he was thrown over backwards. Skipper Gee could not bear to see the prisoners released and the remainder of his Home Guard taken in the rear and scuppered one after the other. He put his hands tightly over his eyes and pressed them hard.

That was how his daughter found him when she brought his tea in the morning.

Straightaway Skipper Gee called a meeting of his Platoon Commanders and said that greater precautions must be taken against attack by Tanks.

" It's no good," said Snowgood Phease, " if we stop 'em using the roads they'll just come across country," but old Guesser Ferrit wrinkled his brow and said " I guess I'll set a few traps for 'em." TRAPS ! That was the solution his anxious brain was looking for ! Gee had not been able to forget the trim camouflaged **Tank** which had appeared so swiftly spitting death in front of it and repelling everyone by its look of deadly efficiency. The armament of the Bloodford Home Guard seemed so slight as to be hopeless against such an instrument of destruction. But here was the magic word— " TRAPS ! "

Point No. 7.
MAKE SOME TANK TRAPS
All sorts of Tank Traps can be devised by anyone with a cunning mind and some of them do not take much making. In siting them do not forget to approach your defences from the way the enemy will come and say to yourself " Where shall I cross this obstacle ? " When you have decided, **that** is where to put your trap.

If necessary make the other possible crossings look a bit more formidable and so help the enemy to decide on the right one.

Eagerly the Skipper heard the old poacher describe how he would make a tank trap at the Ford. He would borrow the digger from the County Council and dig a hole ten feet deep in the river bed, then six inches below the water level he would stretch canvas and put mud on it. To make it look really shallow he would put here and there sods on the canvas with long grass to grow up above the water. " And then," explained Guesser Ferrit, " when the sods get on it they will go straight through to the bottom of the hole." " But what is the use of putting the sods on if they go straight through ? " asked the Skipper. " I mean the *sods* in the Tank ! " said Guesser.

Point No. 8.
FOSTER COMPETITION
There is nothing soldiers enjoy more than friendly competition. If opportunities are afforded for different sections or platoons to see each other's ideas and progress, a spirit of rivalry will be fostered.

So it was decided to start at once on the Tank traps and very ingenious they were. At the Ford the water looked shallower than ever and very tempting for a Tank to cross. At the cutting on Wallop Road, Molotoff Cocktails were hidden, together with a couple of old wagons in the wood ready for pushing into the cutting. Windy Sugden had a bright idea and got permission to dam up CUT BROOK, flooding the marsh right up to the bridge at the bottom of POPPIT HILL. Not to be outdone Snowgood Phease got his men to work and deepened the brook NORTH of the road until it became a perfect tank obstacle and the farmer beamed with delight to see his drainage improved. In one or two places he put wire netting with turf and soil on to tempt tanks to cross just where the channel was deepest. Such was the amused interest taken in these traps by the Home Guard that the Skipper was encouraged to dig pits in gaps in hedges and camouflage them carefully.

Point No. 9.
IMPROVE THE EXISTING OBSTACLES
In a defence scheme, all existing obstacles, both natural and artificial, should be developed and improved. Very little effort can sometimes create magnificent obstacles.

HAG'S POND was enlarged in two places to prevent tanks passing between it and the houses.

One night before going to bed Skipper Gee put these improvements on his map (No. 2) and as he was very tired he soon fell asleep. Then came :—

DREAM NUMBER THREE

Point No. 10.

WATCH FOR THE FIFTH COLUMN

Says Skipper Gee :—

" **The** bland way in which we assume there are no Fifth Column people in this country, is absolutely astounding. They are all over the place abusing our hospitality and taking advantage of our trustful simplicity.

" Let us do two things—not leave a single opening for them to do us down and, above all, let us cultivate suspicious minds so that we can catch them when they come snooping round."

A windy night with dense black clouds riding overhead across the moon. Gee saw someone walking in a furtive way over the Green towards Windy Sugden's tool shed, which was now used as the Home Guard's Ammunition Store. Because one of the Guard had had an accident the Skipper had withdrawn all the S.A.A. and had it kept here under lock and key. Skipper Gee went closer. Surely the man could not be trying to unlock the doors ? This was impudence, who on earth could be doing this at dead of night ? Suddenly a square of ultra blackness appeared in the shadow—the doors were open ! Gee knew what that creaking meant—it was the truck on which the S.A.A. stood, being moved ! Out it came, pushed by that black sinister figure, the boxes of S.A.A. dimly discernible in the darkness.

Suddenly footsteps were heard approaching. Like a flash the truck was pulled back into the shed and the doors were drawn to. An aromatic whiff struck Gee's nostrils and Snowgood Phease drawing comfortably on a cigar came strolling along. He had to pass within a yard of the shed door. Even Snowgood would surely see that padlock hanging loose ! But no, dreamily past it he went ; his cigar giving a derisive gleam. Strain as he would poor Gee could not utter a sound and Snowgood's footfalls faded away. Then slowly, very slowly, the doors were opened, out came the truck, that hateful figure with quick efficiency re-padlocked the door and, pushing hard, went rapidly off into the night.

Reluctant, but fascinated, the Skipper followed on right down to the river. There was a loud splash, gone was the truck, gone was the ammunition and only a few distorted ripples spread across the moving waters.

Speechless with fury Gee ran after the Saboteur but lost him in the darkness. Consumed with apprehension, knowing full well the attack would come at dawn, all night long Skipper Gee went from door to door knocking with all his might but no sound ever came from his blows and no door ever opened.

When a rosy glow tinged the troubled Heavens the dreaded signal came from the WINDMILL and the Church Bells started their clangour. How quickly the Guard turned out ! How clean and well oiled their rifles looked as they fell in outside the Store. Windy Sugden ran out with the key, unlocked the doors and swung them open. There was a horrified incredulous pause and then sudden realization. The ammunition was gone ! Enemies were coming from all sides and not a round of S.A.A. between them !

" Search every house in BLOODFORD ! " yelled Windy, " I'll crucify the bastard that's done this ! " " Why in Heaven's name didn't we keep a guard on it ? " and finally in a pathetic husky voice he said " What shall we do ? " Just then a dozen angry hornets buzzed across the square and the tat-tat-tat-tat of a distant machine gun followed a moment later.

Guesser Ferrit said " Well, I guess I'll fight if it's only with Molotoffs ; come on chaps ! " and away he went to his road block.

A few minutes later half the Home Guard were lined up as prisoners and the other half lay in various parts of the village. Meanwhile the German Officers were talking to a leering, simpering civilian who was telling them a good tale with obvious gusto.

Skipper Gee recognized the furtive figure and with a sudden burst of unutterable fury he flung himself upon him, his eager fingers reaching for his throat—only to find himself on the bedroom floor with the morning sun streaming in through the open windows.

After that the ammunition was moved to the Village Police Station and Gee thought out a number of other ways in which that slinking, black figure could betray the Home Guard and took steps accordingly.

Every day he improved his defences, all the men of his Company fired on the home-made range behind WINDMILL HILL and their performance was good, in fact some were actually marksmen. Range cards were made for the various posts and objects were put at known distances so that they would know the range to any enemy in hitting distance almost as soon as they spotted him. Tank defences proceeded merrily and Gee began to get really satisfied with his plans. Then one night came :—

DREAM NUMBER FOUR

Once again Skipper Gee saw his Home Guard in the middle of a battle, but something was wrong ! A deadly fire was pouring into the village, driving the defenders under cover away from their posts and making it impossible for anyone to move a yard. The enemy was on WINDMILL HILL ! Plenty of cover up there and an easy approach from the North where not a shot could be fired at them ! Gee saw at once what had happened. Why in Heaven's name had he put only three lookout men on the one feature which dominated the whole situation ? With tears running down his cheeks he saw Windy Sugden lead a valiant attack up the bare slopes of the hill. Up they went, giving one another covering fire and advancing by bounds just as he had instructed them, but each advance left behind it a few khaki heaps and it was apparent that the attackers would never reach the top. Like heroes they kept on, but soon the flower of Skipper Gee's Company lay scattered on the green hillside and he saw little parties of Germans spreading out over the fields converging on the village while that deadly searching fire from WINDMILL HILL kept picking off the defenders whenever they showed themselves.

Eight

MAP No. I.

TO WALLOP

WINDMILL HILL

O.P.

OAK WOOD

PIQUET
THE GRANGE

BRIDGE INN

X

TO BEATIT

MARKET HALL

VILLAGE GREEN

PIQUET
DUCK INN

HAG'S POND

X

X

PIQUET
BULL FM.

PINE WOOD

CUT BROOK

TO POPPIT

FORD FM.
PIQUET

RIVER BOOZE

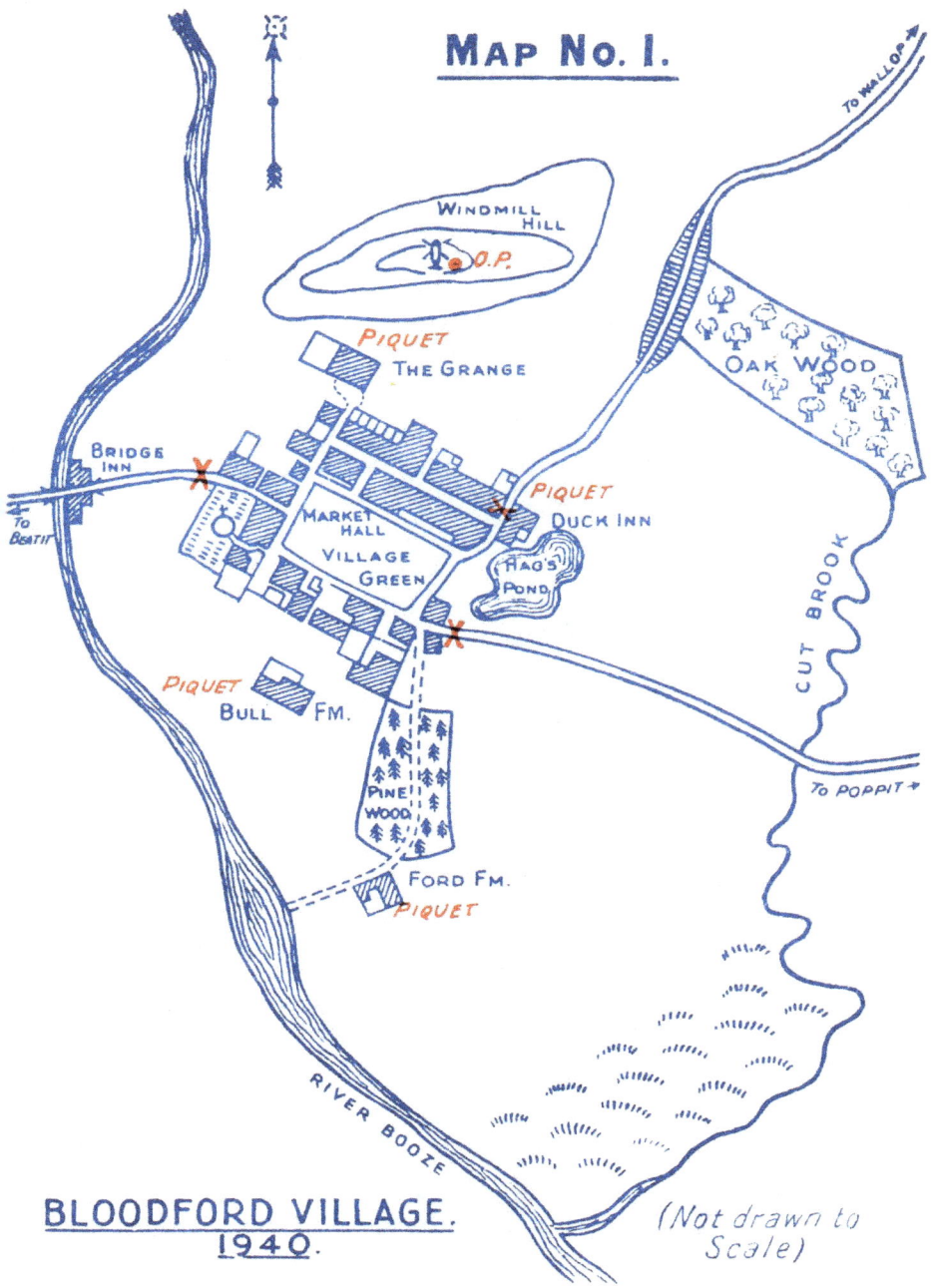

BLOODFORD VILLAGE.
1940.

(Not drawn to Scale)

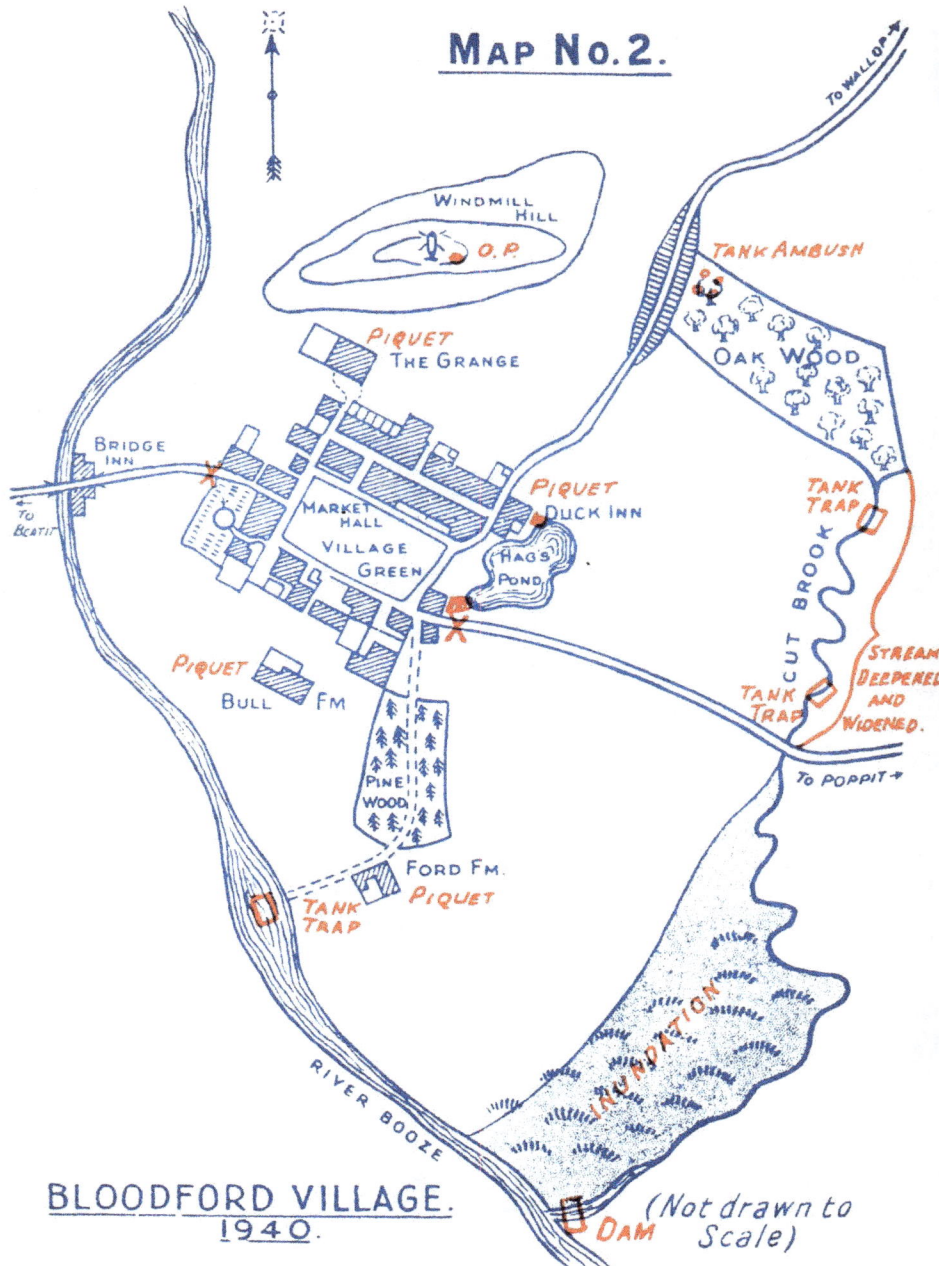

MAP No. 2.

WINDMILL HILL
O.P.

PIQUET THE GRANGE

TANK AMBUSH

OAK WOOD

TO WALLOP →

BRIDGE INN

TO BCATIT

MARKET HALL
VILLAGE GREEN

PIQUET DUCK INN

HAGS POND

TANK TRAP

CUT BROOK

PIQUET BULL FM.

TANK TRAP

STREAM DEEPENED AND WIDENED.

TO POPPIT →

PINE WOOD

FORD FM.
PIQUET

TANK TRAP

INUNDATION

RIVER BOOZE

BLOODFORD VILLAGE.
1940.

(Not drawn to Scale)

DAM

MAP No.3.

WINDMILL HILL

STRONG PIQUET

TO WALLOP

TANK AMBUSH

PIQUET

OAK WOOD

THE GRANGE

BRIDGE INN

TO BSATH

PIQUET
Duck Inn

TANK TRAP

MARKET HALL

VILLAGE GREEN

HAG'S POND

CUT BROOK

TANK TRAP

PIQUET
Bull FM.

TO POPPIT →

PINE WOOD

TANK TRAP

Ford FM.
PIQUET

RIVER BOOZE

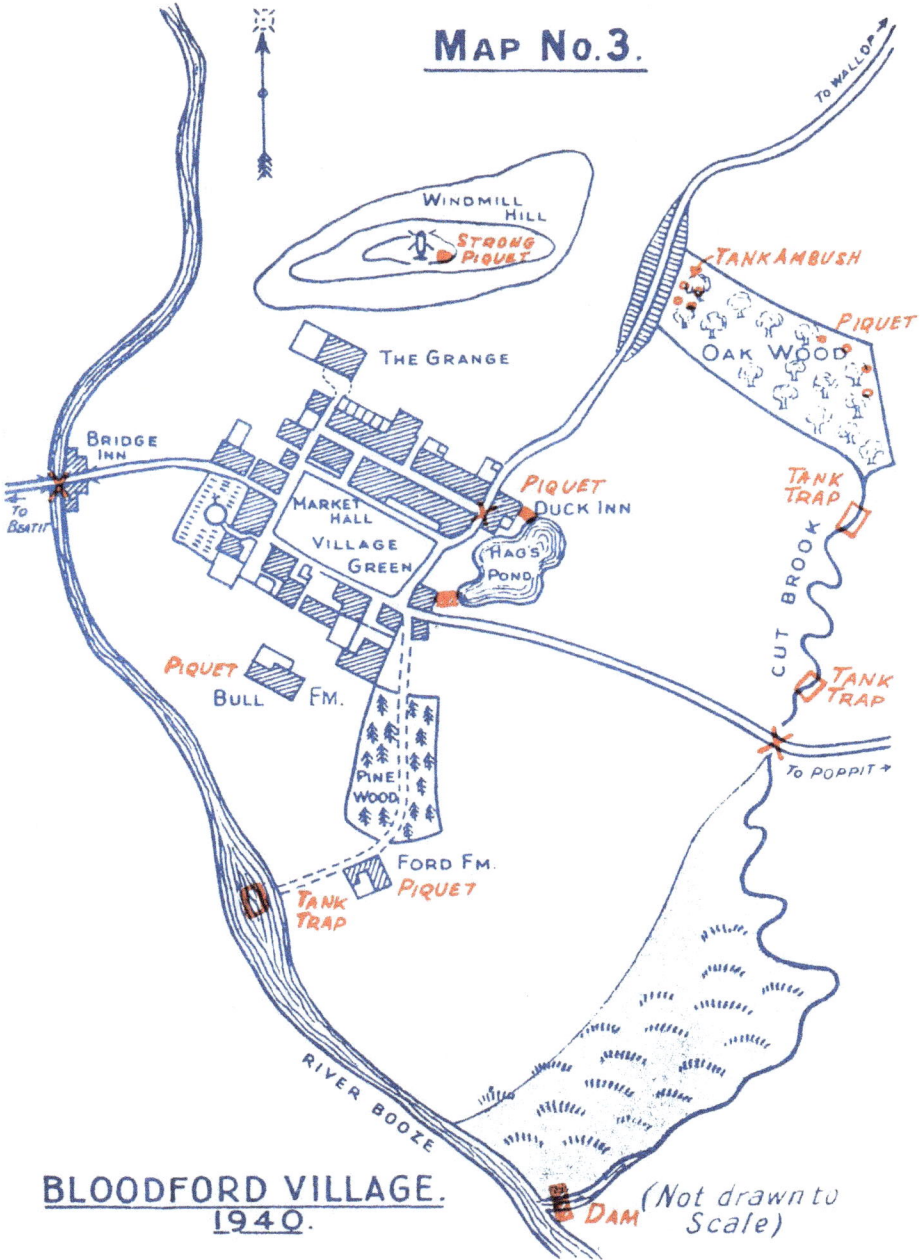

BLOODFORD VILLAGE.
1940.

DAM

(Not drawn to Scale)

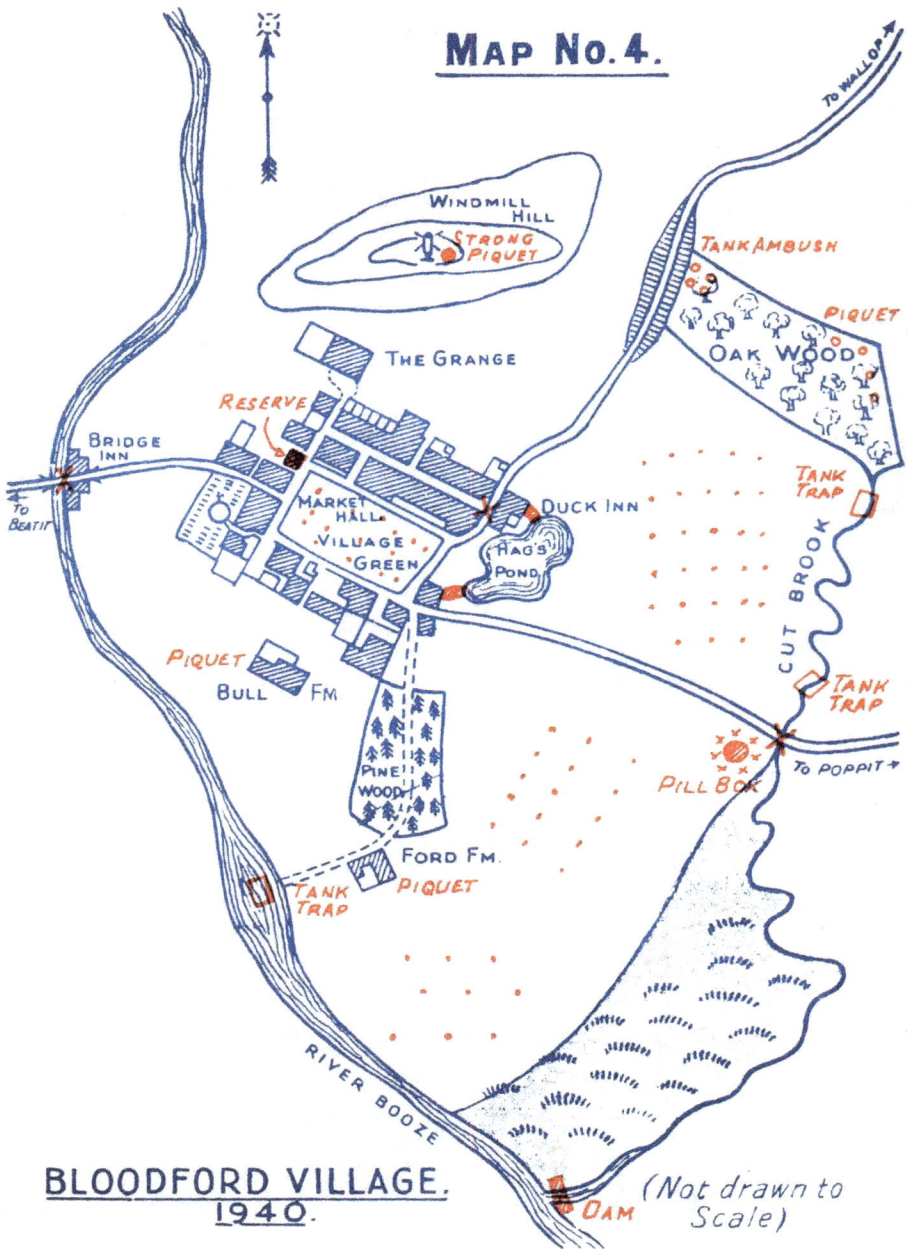

MAP No. 4.

BLOODFORD VILLAGE.
1940.

(Not drawn to Scale)

Labels on map:

- TO WALLOP
- WINDMILL HILL
- STRONG PIQUET
- TANK AMBUSH
- PIQUET
- OAK WOOD
- THE GRANGE
- RESERVE
- BRIDGE INN
- TO BEATIT
- MARKET HALL
- VILLAGE GREEN
- DUCK INN
- HAG'S POND
- TANK TRAP
- CUT BROOK
- PIQUET
- BULL FM.
- TANK TRAP
- PINE WOOD
- PILL BOX
- TO POPPIT
- FORD FM.
- PIQUET
- TANK TRAP
- RIVER BOOZE
- DAM

" This is all my fault ! " whispered Gee to himself. " They trusted me and made me their leader and now they are dying and dead because I let them down ; because I never thought of that simple thing : to occupy the dominant tactical feature ! "

Point No. 13.
OCCUPY THE DOMINANT POINT

Usually in a locality is found some feature such as a hill, building, wood, or even a mound which dominates the surroundings.

At all costs the enemy must be prevented from occupying this spot, in fact, it should form the basis of the Defence Scheme.

Look for it carefully, for, strange though it may seem, the dominant position is not always obvious at first glance.

When he woke up it was with the firm determination to alter his dispositions that very day and to put WINDMILL HILL in such a state of defence that short of an artillery bombardment the enemy could not capture it.

His Defence Scheme was then as shown on Map No. 3. In preparing this he thought of one or two improvements, for instance, he moved the road block from Churchyard Corner to the Bridge, partly because he was afraid of tanks getting over the Bridge and turning off the road NORTH or SOUTH and partly because he considered the Bridge a good place for a road block because it could be easily defended by Molotoff Cocktail Artists from the upstairs of the Inn and the lofts of the stables. Guesser Ferrit also wanted it there because if a tank was turned back at the Bridge it would be ten to one he would try to get over the FORD and he guessed that was where his trap would get " summat in it ! "

The Road Block S.E. of the Square was moved to the Bridge over CUT BROOK and it was decided to occupy the NORTH side of OAK WOOD.

Skipper Gee felt happier now and was losing his careworn look, but a week later came :—

DREAM NUMBER FIVE

Point No. 14.
BLOCK THE LANDING GROUNDS

No Defence Scheme is complete if enemy Troop Carriers can land inside the Defences. It is quite easy to block all possible landing grounds. Old farm carts filled with earth, really stout posts well sunk into the ground, dead trees, old pit ropes stretched across, rollers and various old vehicles are just the thing.

Failing these trenching can be resorted to but if this is done every care should be taken to see that they do not provide for the enemy a covered approach to the defences.

The battle was over ! After a terrific fight the last of the encircling Germans had held up their hands and were now locked in Windy Sugden's shed ! The post on WINDMILL HILL had signalled " No enemy in sight." All round lay evidences of the combat and already the boys were running about wearing German Tin Hats. The women and children had crept out of the cellars and were now on the Green bandaging and refreshing their heroes of the Home Guard, who were strutting about like turkey-cocks, shouting and laughing. Skipper Gee longed to speak to them, to say how proud he too was and how magnificent they had been, but could not utter a sound. But there *was* a sound ! Yes, a swishing, swooping, roaring sound ! Every face on the Green suddenly looked up towards HAG'S POND and with a sweep a huge camouflaged aeroplane skimmed the water, bounced across the Green, knocked over a number of people, and came to a stop. Instantly two machine guns opened fire and a crowd of grey figures swarmed from the 'plane and advanced on the remains of the Home Guard, firing from the hip with light machine guns.

Sick at heart Skipper Gee thought of all the things which could have smashed up that 'plane had they been put on the Village Green, a very little labour would have prevented the tragedy which came in the moment of victory.

" Too late ! " he cried bitterly as he watched the Germans going through the pockets of the dead Home Guards.

" Always too —— ! " and then he found himself awake and realized with a burst of deep thankfulness it was *NOT* too late !

After that, good beefy poles appeared blocking not only the village green but two or three other likely places on the surrounding landscape.

Not trifling sticks but really hefty tree trunks well dug in, nothing less would satisfy Skipper Gee, for he could not forget how enormous the Troop Carrier in his dream had seemed as it swept from the Heavens.

" At last I can go to bed without dreading what I may dream," said Gee and he was still chuckling about some dummy pillboxes which old Guesser Ferrit had distributed round the defences when sleep overtook him.

Point No. 15.
DRAW THE ENEMY'S FIRE !

Put some dummies about to draw the enemy's fire. Remember, ammunition will be more precious than gold to an invader far from his Base, so that every round you can induce him to waste is ONE LESS FOR YOU !

Also, when he fires, he gives away his position, which gives the Defence every chance to retaliate effectively.

DREAM NUMBER SIX

The Battle had been on for some time. Periodic rifle fire could be heard from all the Posts together with the tat-tat-tat-tat of the German machine guns.

Skipper Gee had been wandering round the defences ever since the first alarm and had already seen some very encouraging " scraps." Although the enemy had come in larger numbers than had been anticipated and shown great determination, the Home Guard had thrown them back in grand style.

A glow of pride filled Gee's breast, but he still felt anxious, the enemy were pressing so hard. Every man of the village Home Guard had his job and was at his post. The women and children were under cover, not a soul could be seen in the Square or the streets.

Yet who were these men coming in at the far corner ? A little group of Germans who had worked round the post at BULL FARM, only eight of them under a young Officer, and their sorry plight showed how desperately they had been fighting. Their uniforms were torn and bloodstained and they were so weary they could hardly stagger along. Seeing the Square was empty they threw their arms down and gathered round the pump, some sitting on the ground in utter exhaustion and others washing their wounds and eagerly drinking. " Good God ! " cried Gee. " Why doesn't someone scupper them ? Just a few men could do it now, but in a minute or two they'll be ready to fight again and every man has a sub-machine gun ! "

And then his heart turned to ice because he remembered that not a man of the Home Guard was available for attacking the enemy who had broken through because he, Skipper Gee, had given them all tasks and had not kept even a few men for counter-attack purposes !

Bitterly he uttered the lament of defeated leaders throughout the ages : " Oh, if I had only kept a few men in reserve ! "

Point No. 16.

KEEP A RESERVE

This is of tremendous importance for every Defence Scheme seems weak in parts and the temptation to employ every available man in the initial stages must be sternly resisted.

When the attack is taking place, the reserves should be used only to re-establish the defences if they are penetrated. Once this is done, they should return *at once* to reserve.

Suddenly the German Officer pulled himself up, barked out an order and in spite of their wounds and exhaustion the men sprang to attention. With reluctant admiration Gee saw the officer issue his orders and the men proceed stealthily to attack the Home Guard in the rear. Soon it was all over and Skipper Gee found himself wishing bitterly that *he* was one of those still figures which lay with wax-like faces. They, at least, were unable to dream, unable to suffer any more, unable to reproach themselves unceasingly for failure in a sacred duty !

Skipper Gee did not know it, but this was the *last of his dreams*.

The days which followed produced a marked change in the Defence Scheme. Fortunately for everyone Skipper Gee pushed on with the improvements for all he was worth. Snowgood Phease said it was his opinion a Reserve would be no good because it would never be where it was wanted, but Ferrit guessed it might come in handy. Skipper Gee insisted on the Reserve being formed because, you see, he KNEW ! The Reserve was to be stationed at the detached house at North corner of the square because it was capable of all-round defence, so could act as a keep if the enemy broke in and from there any part of the defences could be reached quickly.

Point No. 17.

ALL-ROUND DEFENCE

The Reserve should be in a place which can, if necessary, act as a Keep and which is capable of all-round defence. Then, if there is a break through on a serious scale, the Reserve will not be suddenly overwhelmed and can make a sortie when it wishes.

The Golden Principle of All-round Defence should apply to *every* *defensive* position no matter how small.

The Enemy cannot take you in the flanks or rear if you haven't got any !

Just as he finished his Defence Scheme his heart was gladdened by the arrival of a brand new Browning Automatic Rifle. This treasure was handed round and much admired by the Bloodford Home Guard. Of course every Platoon and every post had a very good reason why it should be issued to THEM and every man decided that HE was the man to operate it ; but, Gee made up his mind on two things. Firstly, that without fear or favour he would personally choose the most suitable men, cool headed with mechanical aptitude, and secondly that it would be stationed with the RESERVE so that sudden fire power could be developed in any emergency.

For better or worse his dispositions were finally made as shown on Map No. 4.

Then came the day of the Battle. No dream this, but REALITY in its starkest form :—

THE BATTLE

Like all Battles it showed remarkable cussedness in not developing as expected. To begin with, instead of happening at dawn it started at 3 o'clock in the afternoon—a most inconvenient time for the Bloodford Home Guard, the members of which were distributed about their many avocations.

Old Guesser Ferrit was busy destroying wasps' nests with gunpowder behind OAK WOOD ; Snowgood Phease was earnestly dissuading a bellicose client from legal proceedings ; Windy Sugden was out ploughing and Skipper Gee, be it confessed, was fast asleep in his arm chair.

Point No. 18.

HAVE A GOOD SYSTEM OF ALARM

Be satisfied that every man knows how the Alarm will be given and what he is expected to do when it *is* given.

Suddenly old Ferrit heard a large number of aeroplanes approaching and saw scores of parachutes up in the blue void. Quickly he stuck a length of fuse into the gunpowder canister, lit it and dashed behind a tree just as an enormous explosion broke the stillness of the afternoon. Everyone within a couple of miles heard the sound and stood gazing towards where a white plume of smoke was rising into the sky behind OAK WOOD. Then they saw Guesser's figure burst from the wood and heard the faint distant cry of " Stand to ! Stand to ! the Home Guard ! " A minute later the Church Bells gave out their warning and men were rushing from the fields and the houses to draw their arms and ammunition. There was a terrific pounding of hooves and Windy Sugden, astride a heavy carthorse, arrived at the post of duty. Snowgood Phease rushed out of his house with six-and-eightpence in one hand and his rifle in the other. Skipper Gee was on the scene in a matter of seconds, dressed in his Denim uniform, no longer gripped by hideous nightmares but a free man able to order and act.

Point No. 19.

MAN ROAD BLOCKS QUICKLY

On alarm Road Blocks should be manned at the double because the enemy will endeavour to rush them and a few seconds may make all the difference. All traffic should be treated with intense suspicion and kept well away from the Block till its innocence has been established.

The smoke about OAK WOOD had hardly dispersed before the various detachments were on their way. Even then the guard for the BRIDGE ROAD BLOCK arrived only just in time, for coming over the bridge were three civilians on bicycles. They were called upon to halt but hardly seemed to understand ; in fact, they were close to the Road Block before they finally stopped. One of the Guard went out to see their identity cards and had almost got to them when with lightning swiftness they produced ugly-looking Mauser pistols. However, they had not reckoned on Gee's standard of training for the instant their weapons appeared and before they could even lift them up, six triggers were squeezed, six reports rang out as one, and the cyclists were bowled over like rabbits. The Guard had not intended to take any chances and had had them covered all the time.

Point No. 20.
SUSPECT YOUR " SUSPECTS ! "

Whenever anyone is challenged, the challenger should be in readiness to send the challengee to Glory in a split second if he proves hostile. Challenging is often done so casually that if the person challenged produced a pistol instead of an identity card the challenging Home Guard would be completely flummoxed ! That is no sort of soldiering !

Picking up the pistols the sentry returned to the Road Block and this was first blood to the Home Guard !

In the meantime Skipper Gee had been using his glasses and scouting round to find out from which direction the main attack was likely to develop. Things seemed to be happening North of WINDMILL HILL and there was also regular firing from OAK WOOD to the POPPIT ROAD. " Seems suspiciously quiet on the West Side," said Gee, " I'll go along there." When he arrived he looked over the Road Block, saw the three dead Germans lying there with the flies already buzzing round them, and then, looking down the BEATIT ROAD he saw a tiny sparkle amongst some bushes half a mile away. Getting his glasses on this he saw a Tank, its camouflage almost lost in the foliage. The lid of the conning-tower was open and a man was carefully studying the Bridge through binoculars. " We must scare him off so that he will try the Ford," said Gee. " Quick, put a dozen Molotoff Cocktails where he can see them all ready ! Now light one and throw it on the Bridge where he can see it ! Good ! Now nine hundred yards Enemy Tank in front three rounds rapid—FIRE ! " Gee saw the lid close down, there was a moment's hesitation and then the Tank slid off in a Southerly direction. Was it going to try the Ford !

The Skipper saw the Tank draw up under cover and apparently study the Ford and the POST at FORD FARM, evidently hesitating to cross. Gee held his breath and felt he could hardly endure the awful suspense. He looked at the Tank, then at the twinkling waters of the Ford and finally at the Farm. To his surprise he saw a little group of uniformed men leave the farm and run across to the wood in obvious panic. He could not understand this for Young Ferrit was in command there and he was nearly as tough an egg as his father, and then the truth suddenly dawned ! The post had seen the Tank and this was a ruse to coax it across ! And it worked ! for the Tank suddenly darted forward in pursuit and in a few seconds was splashing across the Ford just like the one in his dream—but what a difference! The Tank was almost across when without warning it was GONE ! A few colossal bubbles came to the top and burst. A streak of black oil went twisting down the River and that was all.

It was just as well Skipper Gee went straight back to his Command Post, which was with the reserve, for no sooner had he got there than a Boy Scout arrived, stating breathlessly " Father Timms has sent me from BULL FARM to say he had heard that the Road Block Guard at BRIDGE INN has been wiped out, so he is going to retire to the village ! " Skipper Gee's reply, on a half sheet of paper, was almost scornful :—

" Bridge Guard safe. Only fools listen to rumours. THE HOME GUARD NEVER RETIRES ! GEE."

Point No. 21.
KILL ALL RUMOURS
Whenever a battle is on, Rumours float round astonishingly and nearly all of them are rumours which do not help to maintain morale. Consequently be critical of all information, do not be influenced by rumours and make up your mind not to pass them on without confirmation.

A minute or two later the terrible news reached him that a party of Germans had broken past the post on WINDMILL HILL in spite of heavy casualties and were in houses on the North side of DUCK ROW which runs N.W. from the DUCK INN. They were now giving covering fire to an attack on WINDMILL HILL. Quickly the Skipper gave his orders to Guesser Ferrit, who was to take half the reserve (Gee was very tempted to send the lot, but he remembered something !), scupper the enemy in DUCK ROW and come back into reserve the moment they had done it. Napoleon could not have issued better orders than Guesser's ! His four best marksmen he sent to get on the roof of the Old Market, the highest building in the town. They had orders to snipe any enemy showing at the windows in DUCK ROW and to keep a look out in all directions for any signs of attack upon Ferrit's party while they were clearing the street. Guesser divided the remainder of his party into two parts—one with the Browning rifle to give covering fire and the other to work up the enemy's side of the street. " Why up the enemy's side of the street ? " queried one stalwart. " I guess they will have to lean right out of the windows to shoot at you, which will give us a chance at *them*," said the old Keeper. He also ordered that no one was to advance up the street unless the covering party was letting rip.

Point No. 22.
STREET FIGHTING
If you keep to the side of the street the enemy is holding, he will have to lean right out of the window to shoot at you. This gives your covering fire a chance. Usually you will find most enemy on the right side of the street, so put your covering party on the left and advance on the right. Put some good marksmen on the highest roofs. Send scouts in front of the attacking party and also leave scouts in the rear. If you *can* attack through backyards and gardens instead of up the street, it is usually better to do so. Do not advance till covering fire is all ready to give protection.

As soon as the marksmen on the Old Market had signalled " All ready," Guesser looked round the corner of the Market into DUCK ROW and almost immediately a bullet crashed by his head. Two or three shots sounded above him, and, peeping round again, Guesser had the extreme pleasure of seeing a large German soldier, rifle in hand, somersaulting down to earth from an upstairs window. Confident in the ability of the men above to cover his advance, Guesser led his party round the corner. There the men he had detailed took up positions to give more covering fire, and he and the remainder dashed up the street and started mopping up the houses. Although he lost three men before he was through, his party killed or wounded seven and captured the remainder.

He was back, flushed with victory, in just twenty minutes, and Skipper Gee was very glad to have him and his men in reserve again, for things were hotting up elsewhere. A tank had come down the road from POPPIT and been halted by the Road Block over the CUT BROOK. Unfortunately, however, the pill box which defended this Road Block had not been very well sited, and although the defenders could fire at the Tank they had been unable to prevent some of the Tank's crew from getting out, creeping along the road and taking cover behind the Block itself.

What they were doing Gee could not see but he thought they were fixing an explosive charge. Hastily he sent Ferrit and six men to occupy the two houses at the Southern corner of the Square. Molotoff Cocktails had already been installed in the upstairs rooms and the party went at the double. No sooner were they there than they heard an explosion and the Tank came flying down the road, bumped over the crater where the Road Block had been, passed under their windows so quickly that only one Molotoff struck it at the extreme back.

And there it was, an enemy tank standing right in the heart of their village stronghold !
Then happened the wonderful deed of valour which earned for old Guesser the most coveted of all decorations. At first they thought he had gone mad with rage, for although he could not possibly hit the tank he suddenly started hurling Molotoffs as fast as he could on the Village Green. One after the other he threw them until there was a huge blaze and the smoke drifting right across hid the tank and everything else from view.

When the smoke died down there was Guesser Ferrit standing on top of the tank, striking the cover with a large pick and yelling, " Come out you . . . ! " While everyone gazed spellbound he bashed away till at last up came the lid, and when a German helmet appeared Guesser brought his pick down on it with such a resounding clang that the shaft broke off. As the German fell back into the tank Guesser lost his balance and toppled in after him ! Then what sounds issued from the tank ! Savage imprecations in what seemed like Guesser's voice, falsetto screams, deep grunts and squeals. Finally all was quiet and the spectators held their breath in suspense. What had happened inside ? Were they all dead ?

And then Ferrit's battered old face decorated with a huge purple eye, popped out of the top and a panting voice said, " Somebody come and pull these . . . s out of here ! " Twice had the reserve saved the day.

Point No. 26.
ATTACK THE ATTACKER
" Thrice armed is he who hath his quarrel just !
But six times he who gets his blow in fust ! "
Home Guards ! According to the Poet you can be nine times armed if you seize your opportunity to ATTACK THE ATTACKERS.

Point No. 27.
USE CUNNING
Do not oppose a Tank with Brute Force because that is just what it wants you to do. No, for Heaven's sake use a bit of cunning and from the moment you establish contact with it SHADOW IT. HAUNT IT, HARASS IT, CHASE IT, AND FOOL IT, but make it a Point of **Honour** never to lay off it till it is in one of your traps or you have applied the A. W. Bombs which will seal its doom.

The third tank was easy meat. It came from the East, nosed along CUT BROOK till it found one of the camouflaged traps, thought it could get across, and down it went ! It thrashed about, its tracks going deeper and deeper in the mud till the CUT BROOK was lost in blue fumes and the crew were gassed out. Snowgood Phease had been watching the Tank's struggles, and as the suffocating crew climbed out he said, " It's no good letting 'em escape," and shot them one after the other.

Point No. 28.
GET THE RIGHT IDEA ABOUT TANKS
Says old Guesser Ferrit :—
" People looks at Tanks all wrong. It's no use lookin' at a Tank wot's comin' and saying, ' Here comes a bloody Juggernaut wot nobody can stop ! ' 'cos that's all tripe.
" To me a German Tank comin' along is nuthin' but a little group of MEN, anxious, worried, half-suffocated MEN, cooped up in misery, every minute dreading an anti-tank gun and their eyes droppin' out of their heads with searchin' the Earth beneath for mines and the Heavens above for dive bombers. In fact, it's a kindness to sneak up and put 'em out of their misery with a Molotoff Cocktail or an A.W. Bomb ! "

With the loss of their tanks the enemy's pressure eased considerably except from the North where they were assembling for another attack. This was reported to Skipper Gee by a Boy Scout, and he ordered men from the Post in OAK WOOD to deploy in the sunken road and attack the attacker's flank. That did it. The Bloodford Home Guard made their one and only Bayonet charge. And Boy ! Did they enjoy it ?

An hour after the last shot had been fired and the last prisoner brought in, an English 'plane went over and dropped a message on the village Green. It was from Command Headquarters and said : " HOLD ON AT ALL COSTS. HELP IS COMING."

It was passed round, and when it reached Old Guesser Ferrit he spelt it out painstakingly, spat upon the grass, and said, " I guess the Bloodford Home Guard don't need no help from nobody ! "